GRAYSCALE
COLORING BOOK

WONDERFUL LADYBUGS AND FLOWERS

ADULT
COLORING BOOK

VOLUME 3.

PATTERNS FOR RELAXATION AND STRESS RELIEF

COLOR TEST PAGE

www.ingramcontent.com/pod-product-compliance
Lightning Source LLC
Chambersburg PA
CBHW052015280526
45793CB00005B/985
* 9 7 8 1 5 3 6 9 5 3 7 5 6 *